D1399774

VATICAN CITY

Shenaaz Nanji

www.av2books.com

AV² provides enriched content that supplements and complements this boo[k]
Weigl's AV² books strive to create inspired learning and engage young min[ds]
in a total learning experience.

Your AV² Media Enhanced books come alive with...

Audio
Listen to sections of the book read aloud.

Key Words
Study vocabulary, and complete a matching word activity.

Go to **www.av2books.com**, and enter this book's unique code.

Video
Watch informative video clips.

Quizzes
Test your knowledge.

BOOK CODE

W 7 1 7 4 4 7

Embedded Weblinks
Gain additional information for research.

Slide Show
View images and captions, and prepare a presentation.

AV² by Weigl brings you media enhanced books that support active learning.

Try This!
Complete activities and hands-on experiments.

... and much, much more[!]

Published by AV² by Weigl
350 5th Avenue, 59th Floor
New York, NY 10118
Websites: www.av2books.com   www.weigl.com

Library of Congress Cataloging-in-Publication Data
Nanji, Shenaaz, author.
 Vatican City / Shenaaz Nanji.
     pages cm. -- (Houses of faith)
 Includes index.
 ISBN 978-1-4896-1158-1 (hardcover : alk. paper) -- ISBN 978-1-4896-1159-8 (softcover : alk. paper) -- ISBN 978-1-4896-1160-4 (single user ebk.) -- ISBN 978-1-4896-1161-1 (multi user ebk.)
 1. Church buildings--Vatican City--Juvenile literature. 2. Vatican City--Juvenile literature. 3. Vatican City--History--Juvenile literature. 4. Vatican City--Buildings, structur[es,] etc.--Juvenile literature. I. Title. II. Series: Houses of faith.
 NA5620.A1N36 2014
 945.6'34--dc23
                    2014002105

Editor: Heather Kissock
Design: Mandy Christiansen

Printed in the United States of America in North Mankato, Minnesota
1 2 3 4 5 6 7 8 9 0 18 17 16 15 14

032014
WEP150314

Every reasonable effort has been made to trace ownership and to obtain permission to reprint copyright material. The publishers would be pleased to have any errors or omissions brought to their attention so that they may be corrected in subsequent printings. Weigl acknowledges Getty Images, Alamy, Newscom, and Dreamstime as its primary image suppliers for this title.

Contents

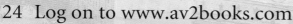

What Is Vatican City?

Nestled in the heart of Rome, Italy, is an independent **city-state** called Vatican City. This small city is home to the **seat** of the Roman Catholic Church. Its leader, the pope, lives here, and all major decisions regarding the Roman Catholic faith are made within the city walls.

Much of Vatican City was built between the 14th and 17th centuries. During this period, called the **Renaissance**, there was a revival and rebirth of art, architecture, and learning in Europe. Many of the structures in Vatican City reflect the architectural styles of the time.

Vatican City covers less than 0.5 square miles (1.3 square kilometers), but it features several well-known buildings and structures. People from all over the world, and of various religions, come to Vatican City to see its beautiful churches, squares, and palaces.

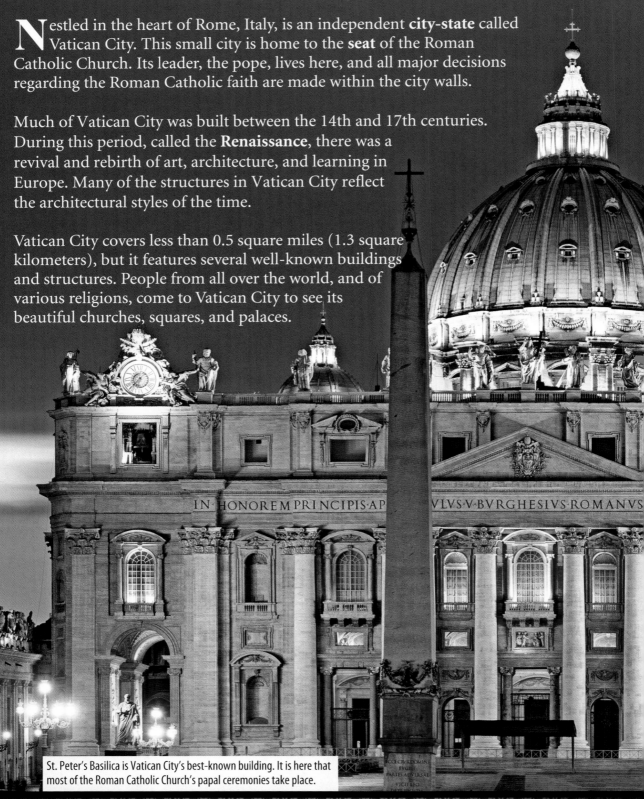

St. Peter's Basilica is Vatican City's best-known building. It is here that most of the Roman Catholic Church's papal ceremonies take place.

The Roman Catholic Faith

Roman Catholicism is a Christian religion. This means it is based on the teachings of Jesus Christ, a man believed to have lived more than 2,000 years ago. Followers of the Roman Catholic faith share several beliefs with other Christians. They believe that Jesus Christ was the Son of God, and they read a book called the Bible for spiritual inspiration. However, Roman Catholicism has several beliefs that are unique. Roman Catholics, for instance, believe that **saints** can cure illnesses and help people in need. They also believe in a place called purgatory that prepares people to enter heaven after they have died.

By 2014, the Roman Catholic Church had been led by **266 popes**.

The Bible was written by at least 40 men. It took approximately **1,600 years** to write it.

1.2 billion
People practice Roman Catholicism worldwide. Roman Catholics are the world's largest Christian group.

Roman Catholics 1.2 Billion+

Protestants 670 Million+

Orthodox 285 Million+

Anglicans 82 Million+

X·AN·MDCXII·PONT·VII

A Step Back in Time

The Vatican City site has had religious connections since Saint Peter, the first pope, used the area as his base. When Peter died, he was buried on a hill just outside Rome. Known as Vatican Hill, it became a sacred site for followers of the Roman Catholic faith. In 326 AD, the Roman Emperor Constantine built a church over the burial site to honor Peter. The church was called Saint Peter's Basilica.

Over the years, steps were taken to protect the basilica from invaders. One of the main developments was the construction of high walls around the church. However, in 1309, the seat of the Roman Catholic Church moved to France. Vatican Hill and St. Peter's Basilica were abandoned for more than 70 years.

CONSTRUCTION TIMELINE

326 AD Emperor Constantine builds a church over the burial site of St. Peter on Vatican Hill.

800s Pope Leo IV begins the construction of walls around Saint Peter's Basilica.

Late 1500s A new Apostolic Palace is built by Pope Sixtus V. Located closer to St. Peter's Basilica, it is where all popes since have lived.

325 AD	800	1200	1400	1600

1200s The first Apostolic Palace is built by Pope Nicholas III. This palace will serve as the home of the pope.

1506 Pope Julius II commissions a major renovation of St. Peter's Basilica. The **cornerstone** is laid in 1506.

1400s Pope Sixtus IV builds the first Vatican Library and **commissions** the building of the Sistine Chapel, which completes construction in 1481.

In 1377, the seat returned to Rome. Repairing the basilica and establishing a home base for the pope became priorities. A construction spurt began that lasted for more than 200 years. New buildings rose around the basilica. These buildings formed what is now called Vatican City.

The papacy moved to France when the French pope Clement V refused to move to Rome. Over time, a papal palace was established in Avignon, France. Popes ruled from this palace until the papacy returned to Rome in 1377.

1626 The renovation of St. Peter's Basilica is completed.

1656 Pope Alexander VII commissions the design and construction of St. Peter's Square, the grand **piazza** in front of St. Peter's Basilica.

2009 In an effort to conserve energy, the city installs Europe's largest solar plant on its grounds.

| 1625 | 1700 | 1800 | 1970 | 2010 |

1667 St. Peter's Square completes construction.

1971 The Paul VI Audience Hall is completed. The building is used when the weather is unsuitable for outdoor ceremonies.

Vatican City's Location

Vatican City was originally across from Rome, on the west bank of the Tiber River. As Rome's population grew, the city expanded across the river and surrounded the small city-state. Today, Vatican City is found just northwest of Rome's center.

AREA The city is believed to cover approximately 0.17 square miles (0.44 sq. km).

BORDER Vatican City's border, including the walls, extends for about 2 miles (3.2 km).

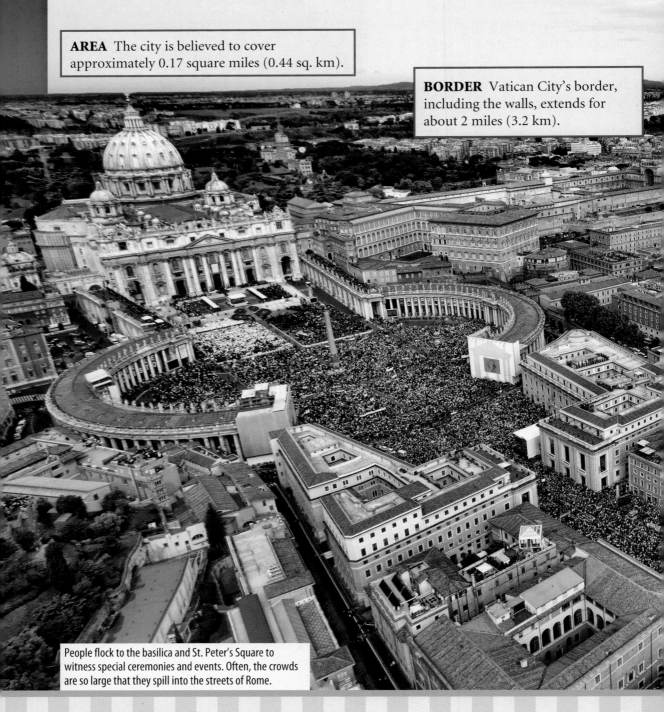

People flock to the basilica and St. Peter's Square to witness special ceremonies and events. Often, the crowds are so large that they spill into the streets of Rome.

The city-state is entirely landlocked. Its border with Rome is marked mostly by walls. The exception is found at St. Peter's Square, where the border between Rome and Vatican City is marked by a painted white line.

ELEVATION Although Vatican City is located on a hill, there is very little variance in elevation. The city's highest point is 248 feet (76 meters) above sea level, and its lowest point is 63 feet (19 m).

LENGTH At its longest point, the city stretches across only 0.6 miles (0.97 km)

WIDTH At its widest point, Vatican City reaches only 0.5 miles (0.81 km).

Vatican City Buildings

Vatican City serves as both a place of worship and an administrative center. Its buildings reflect the importance of the city to the Roman Catholic faith.

ST. PETER'S BASILICA St. Peter's Basilica is one of the largest churches in the world. It measures 614 feet (187 m) long and 459 feet (140 m) wide. The basilica features the main, or papal, **altar**, where the pope conducts **mass**. Several chapels are found around the perimeter of the building. Sculptures, **mosaics**, and other artwork adorn the interior.

APOSTOLIC PALACE Best known as the pope's official residence, the palace is also home to the Vatican Museums, the Vatican Library, and a variety of administrative offices. The Sistine Chapel is also part of the Apostolic Palace. This small church is known for its ceiling. Master artist Michelangelo spent four years painting it with scenes from the Old Testament.

PAUL VI AUDIENCE HALL One of the most recent buildings to be added to Vatican City, the Paul VI Audience Hall lacks the grandeur of Renaissance architecture. In comparison, the modern, **reinforced concrete** building is quite plain. Its curved roof is covered with solar panels. However, the hall's open interior allows for large gatherings of up to 6,300 people. This helps to make it one of the most used buildings in Vatican City.

One of the best-known paintings in the Sistine Chapel is *The Creation of Adam*, which shows God creating the first man.

The mosaics found in St. Peter's often portray events found in the Bible, such as Jesus giving St. Peter the keys of Heaven.

The dome of St. Peter's Basilica was designed by Michelangelo, one of the greatest artists of all time.

People visiting the Vatican Museums often use the spiral staircase. The staircase is made up of two intertwining spirals. One is for people entering the museums. The other is for people leaving.

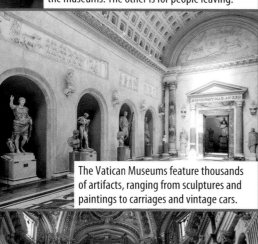

The Vatican Museums feature thousands of artifacts, ranging from sculptures and paintings to carriages and vintage cars.

The Chair of St. Peter sits inside the basilica. Believed to have been used by St. Peter himself, the chair is set inside an elaborate altar.

St. Peter's Basilica has the

LARGEST

interior of any Christian church in the world.

The Apostolic Palace has more than 1,400 rooms.

It would take **4 years** to view all of paintings in the Vatican Museum if **1 minute** was spent viewing each piece.

The Vatican has its own post office and issues its own stamps.

There are no **highways** in the Vatican, only **streets** and **lanes**.

The Vatican Library has almost **1 million** books in its collection.

Vatican City's **railway station** began operating in

1930.

It is mostly used to ship freight.

Vatican City Features

Vatican City has a variety of structures, monuments, and quiet spaces. It also houses some of the world's greatest works of art.

ST. PETER'S SQUARE The enormous piazza of St. Peter's Square sits before the entrance to St. Peter's Basilica. Surrounded by two curving colonnades, the square was built to hold the thousands of worshipers who come to Vatican City for papal blessings. In the center of St. Peter's Square is an 83-foot (25.3 m) tall **obelisk** that is flanked by a fountain on each side. Made from a single piece of red granite, the obelisk weighs more than 350 tons (318 metric tons).

SCULPTURES Sculptures are found throughout Vatican City. The interior of St. Peter's Basilica alone contains more than 40. Others are found in the Vatican Gardens and along the **colonnades** surrounding St. Peter's Square. Pilgrims from all over the world come to see the statue of St. Peter in St. Peter's Basilica. They touch St. Peter's feet and ask for blessings. The Pieta was created by Michelangelo. It shows Jesus Christ's mother, Mary, holding his body after the crucifixion.

GARDENS More than half of Vatican City consists of gardens. Located mainly behind the Apostolic Palace, the gardens feature flower beds, monuments, fountains, and a forest. The area is not open for public viewing, however. People must book tours to walk through the grounds.

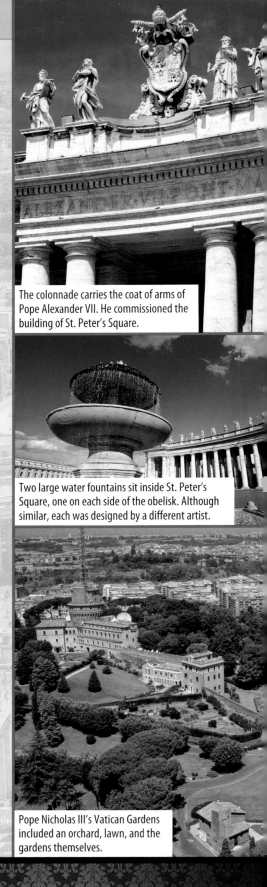

The colonnade carries the coat of arms of Pope Alexander VII. He commissioned the building of St. Peter's Square.

Two large water fountains sit inside St. Peter's Square, one on each side of the obelisk. Although similar, each was designed by a different artist.

Pope Nicholas III's Vatican Gardens included an orchard, lawn, and the gardens themselves.

The obelisk acts as a sundial. Its shadows are cast on markings found on the square's stonework.

Michelangelo was only 24 years old when he sculpted the Pieta.

The **Pieta** was sculpted from a single piece of marble.

In **1279,** the first gardens in Vatican City were planted by Pope Nicholas III.

Fewer than **1,000 people** live in Vatican City.

The obelisk in St. Peter's Square is more than **4,000** years old. It was built for an Egyptian pharaoh.

The Vatican Gardens account for **57 acres** (23 hectares) of the city's land.

Statues of **140 saints** stand on top of the *colonnades* of St. Peter's Square.

There is a heliport in the Vatican Gardens.

The Science behind Vatican City

Building Vatican City was a long and difficult process. The people who built the first structures inside Vatican City did not have power tools to help in the construction process. They had to rely on the knowledge, materials, and technology of the time. It was important that the structures be made of strong materials so that they would last for years to come. However, the **architects** and artists involved in Vatican City's construction also wanted to use materials that could be molded into beautiful shapes and designs.

THE PROPERTIES OF MARBLE Most of the monuments and buildings in Vatican City are made from Carrara marble. This beautiful white and gray-blue marble came from the town of Carrara in the Italian Alps. Marble was a popular choice for building and sculpture during the Renaissance. It is known as a soft rock, meaning that it can be easily cut and shaped. The Mohs measurement of hardness scale determines the hardness of a stone based on how easily it can be scratched by grit. The scale ranges from one to ten, with ten being the hardest stone. Marble has a measurement of three on the scale. Marble's softness allows the rock to be sculpted into beautiful artistic shapes.

CUTTING THE MARBLE To extract the marble from the **quarry**, workers relied on chisels, hammers, and other hand tools. A chisel is a type of simple machine called a wedge. Pointed at one end, it gradually widens to the other end. Workers would place the pointed end of the chisel against the marble and begin to hammer on the wide end. This pressure would force the chisel's point deeper into the rock, allowing the workers to cut the marble into large blocks.

SLEDGING After the marble was cut into blocks, it was ready to be transported from the top of the mountains to the bottom of the valley. In a process called sledging, workers loaded the marble blocks onto a wooden sled that was attached to a system of ropes. Relying on the force of **gravity**, the workers then rolled the sled down the hill by gradually releasing the ropes. The challenge for the workers was to control the speed. They had to keep the marble block moving at a sufficient speed so it would not get stuck in the middle of the hill. At the same time, they also had to prevent the sled from gaining too much speed, or it could overrun the workers and crush them to death.

Marble has been quarried from the mountains around Carrara for more than 2,000 years.

About 1 million tons (907,185 metric tons) of Carrara marble are quarried each year.

Today, sledges have been replaced with modern machinery. This equipment helps to transfer the marble more efficiently than in the past.

Chisels are still used to cut and shape rock.

Vatican City's Builders

Most of the structures in Vatican City are the works of Renaissance artists and architects. Many of these people worked on the same building, St. Peter's Basilica. The basilica's construction was such a long process that no one person was able to supervise the entire project.

Donato Bramante Donato Bramante began his architectural career in Milan, Italy, but his best-known work is found in Rome. It is here that Pope Julius II gave him the job of redesigning Vatican City. Central to this plan was the renovation of St. Peter's Basilica. In true High Renaissance style, Bramante's design for the basilica showed a Greek cross with all four arms of equal length. A grand dome accompanied by several smaller domes and towers were also part of the plan. Bramante died before the construction was completed, but key components of his design were retained in the final building.

Domenico Fontana When Pope Sixtus V decided to have a new Apostolic Palace built in the late 1500s, he chose architect Domenico Fontana for the job. Fontana was well known in the area due to his previous work for the pope. In fact, Fontana was responsible for moving the Egyptian obelisk to the center of St. Peter's Square. He had also designed the Vatican Library and helped supervise the construction of the dome in St. Peter's Basilica. Following his work for the papacy, Fontana moved to Naples, where he became an **engineer**.

Bernini spent nine years working on the baldachin. Made entirely of bronze, it rises 95 feet (29 m) in height and weighs approximately 13,700 pounds (6,200 kg).

Michelangelo In the years following Bramante's death, several architects were charged with overseeing the construction of St. Peter's Basilica. However, it was not until Michelangelo was assigned to supervise its construction that the building began to truly move forward. By this time, Michelangelo was in his seventies and had already achieved much success in his career. He was known for his paintings in the Sistine Chapel and for his many other paintings and sculptures. While some of the previous architects had strayed from Bramante's original design for St. Peter's Basilica, Michelangelo honored the design and developed it further. His greatest contribution to the basilica is the design of the dome.

Carlo Maderno Carlo Maderno was the nephew of Domenico Fontana and **apprenticed** under him. In 1603, Maderno succeeded Michelangelo as the supervising architect of St. Peter's Basilica. Maderno was responsible for designing the basilica's **nave** and **facade**. Today, the balcony on Maderno's facade is where new popes are announced and papal blessings given.

Gian Lorenzo Bernini The final stage of St. Peter's construction was supervised by Gian Lorenzo Bernini. Known as one of the greatest sculptors of the 17th century, Bernini made two major contributions to the papal city. He built the baldachin, a giant bronze canopy, over the main altar of St. Peter's Basilica. He was also responsible for creating the 284-columned colonnade that surrounds St. Peter's Square.

Similar Structures around the World

Renaissance architecture can be found throughout Europe. It is easily recognized by its use of **symmetry** and **geometry**. Renaissance buildings, including churches, often feature elements that originated in the architecture of ancient Greece and Rome. Domes, arches, and columns are common to most Renaissance buildings.

Duomo of Florence

BUILT: 1296–1436 AD
LOCATION: Florence, Italy
DESIGN: Arnolfo di Cambio, Filippo Brunelleschi
DESCRIPTION: Also known as the Basilica di Santa Maria del Fiore, the Duomo is often referred to as the birthplace of the Renaissance. Initially designed to follow the **Gothic** style, the cathedral began to take on more **classical** features during its construction. One of the key features added to the cathedral was its dome. It was this piece that signified the beginning of Renaissance architecture. The dome has no supports underneath it and is made of two layers. The layers work together to support each other and the dome as a whole.

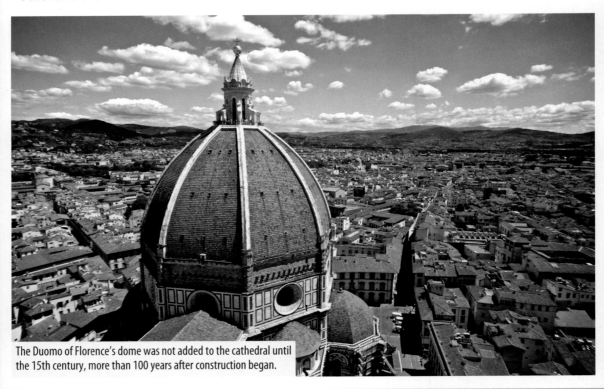

The Duomo of Florence's dome was not added to the cathedral until the 15th century, more than 100 years after construction began.

Church of San Giorgio Maggiore

BUILT: 1566–1610 AD
LOCATION: Venice, Italy
DESIGN: Andrea Palladio
DESCRIPTION: Once the site of a Benedictine monastery, the Church of San Giorgio Maggiore is one of the most prominent buildings in Venice. Located on the island of San Giorgio Maggiore, the basilica's gleaming white marble facade stands in front of the red brick building that houses the actual church. The building pays tribute to Roman architecture, featuring columns, **pediments**, arches, and a dome. Its interior includes a central altar, a series of side chapels, and several important artworks.

The Church of San Giorgio Maggiore is one of the first buildings visitors encounter when they arrive in Venice by sea.

Jaen Cathedral is located in Santa Maria Square, which is considered to be the historic center of the city.

Jaen Cathedral

BUILT: 1540–late 18th century
LOCATION: Jaen, Spain
DESIGN: Andres de Vandelvira
DESCRIPTION: A religious building has stood on the site of Jaen Cathedral for more than 1,000 years. When the **Moors** ruled Spain, it was the site of a **mosque**. Later, a Gothic cathedral was built on the land. The Renaissance cathedral that now sits on the site took more than 300 years to build. Its size is impressive, and it easily looms over the surrounding area. The building itself is rectangular in shape. Inside, columns divide the cathedral into three sections, each containing a series of chapels.

Issues Facing Vatican City

Many of Vatican City's buildings, squares, and sculptures are hundreds of years old. They were built using the best materials of the time. However, the passage of time has created problems for these structures. Many are experiencing wear due to their age and the conditions they experience.

WHAT IS THE ISSUE?

The Sistine Chapel's artwork is being damaged by the approximately 5 million tourists who visit the site every year.

Over time, exposure to the elements has affected the condition of the structures in St. Peter's Square.

EFFECTS

The humidity and dirt generated by tourists cause damaging layers of dirt and dust to accumulate on the paintings.

The columns and statues along the colonnade have lost their vibrant color, and have algae, moss, and lichens growing in some areas.

ACTION TAKEN

A new air conditioning and filtering system was recently installed to help the levels of heat and dirt in the chapel. Officials are also considering the idea of placing a limit on the number of daily visitors allowed inside.

A restoration project to clean and repair the structures began in 2009. The work involved removing algae that had gathered on the stonework and repairing fragments that were in danger of falling from the structures.

Create a Mosaic

Mosaics make up much of the artwork in St. Peter's Basilica. Tiles were preferred over paint because they were longer lasting. Follow the instructions below to make your own mosaic masterpiece.

Materials
- a square aluminum tray
- plaster of Paris
- multicolored craft tiles
- glue
- grout
- plastic spatula
- sponge
- mixing bowl

Instructions

1. Decide what kind of picture you would like to make with your tiles. It could be a favorite animal, your favorite sport, or an interesting pattern.

2. Select tiles in the colors you need to make your picture. Arrange them on the table so that they form the picture you want to make.

3. Use the mixing bowl to make your plaster. Mix enough plaster to fill the tray.

4. Pour the plaster into the tray. Spread it, and let it dry for about an hour.

5. When the plaster is dry, remove it from the tray.

6. Place glue on the back of each tile and transfer the tiles, one by one, to the surface of the plaster. Let your design sit to dry.

7. Mix the grout with water until it is a thick paste.

8. Using the spatula, cover your mosaic with the grout. Be sure to push the grout into the cracks between the tiles. It is fine if the grout covers the tiles.

9. Let your mosaic sit for a few minutes. Then, take a damp sponge and wipe the grout off the surface of the tiles. Show your mosaic to your friends and family.

Vatican City Quiz

Q Why was Vatican City built at this site?

A It was where St. Peter, the first pope, was buried.

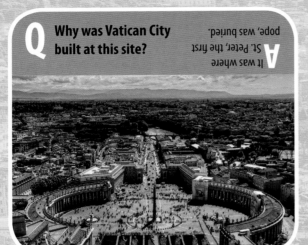

Q During which historical period was much of Vatican City built?

A The Renaissance

Q Who designed the dome in St. Peter's Basilica?

A Michelangelo

Q What type of marble was used in the construction of many of the buildings and monuments in Vatican City?

A Carrara marble

Key Words

altar: an elevated structure where religious ceremonies are performed

apprenticed: assigned to work for someone who is skilled in a trade

architects: people who design buildings

city-state: an independent city that has its own government and does not belong to a country

classical: relating to Greek or Latin culture

colonnades: a series of columns placed at regular intervals

commissions: authorizes the production of something

cornerstone: a foundation stone

engineer: a person who applies scientific principles to the design of structures

facade: the principal front of a building

geometry: a branch of mathematics that deals with measurement

Gothic: a style of architecture popular in Europe from the 12th to 16th centuries

gravity: the force that pulls objects toward the center of Earth

mass: a religious ceremony

Moors: Muslim people from northwest Africa

mosaics: designs made up of tiny colored tiles

mosque: a place of worship for those who follow the Muslim faith

nave: the central part of a church

obelisk: a tall, square-shaped tower capped with a pyramid shape

pediments: triangular areas on the fronts of buildings

piazza: open public space

quarry: a pit from which stone is obtained

reinforced concrete: concrete that has metal bars embedded in it to add strength

Renaissance: a period between the 14th and 16th centuries that saw a revival of classical art, literature, and architecture

saints: people who have been officially recognized as holy by the Church

seat: a center of authority

symmetry: having two sides that look alike

Index

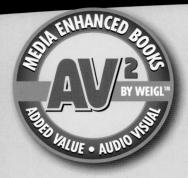

Log on to www.av2books.com

AV² by Weigl brings you media enhanced books that support active learning. Go to www.av2books.com, and enter the special code found on page 2 of this book. You will gain access to enriched and enhanced content that supplements and complements this book. Content includes video, audio, weblinks, quizzes, a slide show, and activities.

AV² Online Navigation

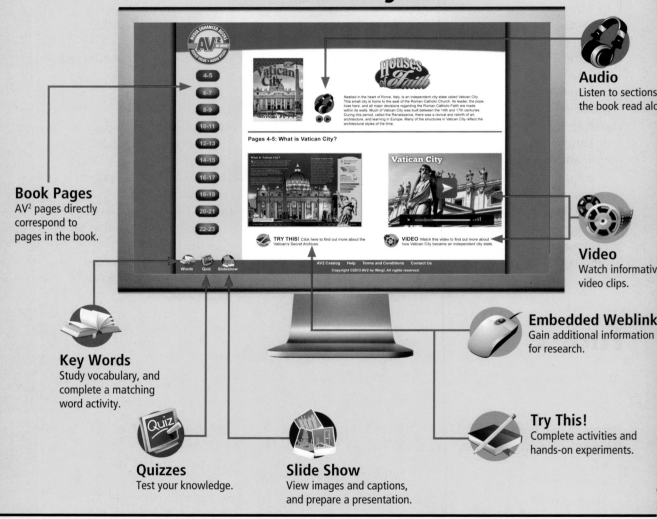

Book Pages
AV² pages directly correspond to pages in the book.

Audio
Listen to sections the book read al[oud]

Video
Watch informativ[e] video clips.

Key Words
Study vocabulary, and complete a matching word activity.

Embedded Weblink[s]
Gain additional information for research.

Quizzes
Test your knowledge.

Slide Show
View images and captions, and prepare a presentation.

Try This!
Complete activities and hands-on experiments.

AV² was built to bridge the gap between print and digital. We encourage you to tell us what you like and what you want to see in the future.

Sign up to be an AV² Ambassador at www.av2books.com/ambassador.

Due to the dynamic nature of the Internet, some of the URLs and activities provided as part of AV² by Weigl may have changed or ceased to exist. AV² by Weigl accepts no responsibility for any such changes. All media enhanced books are regularly monitored to update addresses and sites in a timely manner. Contact AV² by Weigl at 1-866-649-3445 or av2books@weigl.com with any questions, comments, or feedback.